Proper Education Group

4 Practice Tests for the California Driver's Permit Test

"The secret to getting ahead is getting started."
Mark Twain

Table of Contents

Introduction

1.1 License types

You need to understand the available driver's licenses in California solely because for each license type there's a matching type of instruction permit. The licenses include:

Class C	This is the standard kind of driver's license. It permits you to drive common cars: 2-axle vehicles whose gross vehicle weight rating (GVWR) is 26,000 pounds or less. This class includes vans and automobiles with less than 15 occupants, with the driver included.
Class A	Consents you to haul travel trailers whose gross vehicle weight rating (GVWR) surpasses 10,000 pounds, and 5th-wheel travel trailers weighing over 15,000 pounds, as well as any vehicle that a Class C license permits.
Class B	Allows you to tow a single vehicle with a gross vehicle weight rating (GVWR) of 10,000 pounds or less and 5th wheel travel trailers not exceeding 15,000 pounds, as well as any vehicle that a Class C license permits you to drive.
Class M	Allows you to ride a motorized bicycle or scooter, moped, or bicycle with an attached motor.

1.2 Application process

1. You must be at least 18 years old to acquire the Class C California license (the usual kind of driver's license) as explained in the table above.
2. You must have fully finalized and signed the Driver License & ID Card Application (DL 44/eDL 44) form available here https://www.dmv.ca.gov/portal/driver-licenses-identification-cards/dl-id-online-app-edl-44/
3. An instruction permit held for more than six months
4. Evidence of a viable Social Security number: your Social Security card, W-2 form, paycheck displaying your name and SSN, or a signed affidavit asserting you are not eligible for an SSN
5. Proof of legal citizenship in California. Usually a U.S. birth certificate or U.S. passport
6. Proof of identity: U.S. Birth Certificate, U.S. Passport, U.S. Military ID, Permanent Resident Card, foreign passport with a valid I-94 or a Certificate of Naturalization.

What are the requirements for young drivers?

1. Californian minors aged between 15 ½ and 18 who want to acquire a driver's license must first apply for a provisional instruction permit. Their parent(s) or guardian(s) sign the application for them.
2. A completed California Driver's License or Identification (DL/ID) Card Application
3. A certificate of completion of driver education or certificate of enrollment in an integrated (classroom) driver education and driver training program
4. Evidence of financial responsibility: proof of insurance coverage

The younger drivers can then apply for the California DL/ID card once they reach 18 years old.

About the Exam

1. TLSAE course for the new drivers.

One of the license requirements for new California drivers is taking a Traffic Law and Substance Abuse Education Course (TLSAE).https://www.flhsmv.gov/driver-licenses-id-cards/education-courses/driver-improvement-schools/traffic-law-substance-abuse-education-tlsae-find-approved-listing-tlsae-course-providers/

The course can be taken online or in-class, and it provides the essentials of California traffic laws, particularly those related to road safety and alcohol use.

2. Vision test

For the safety of yourself and others, you will need to undertake a vision test before getting your license. The test requires you to pass with or without corrective lenses and have a visual acuity better than 20/200. A minimal corrected visual acuity of 20/70 is required for a restricted license, while a minimal uncorrected visual acuity of 20/40 is required for an unrestricted license.

3. Knowledge exam

Once you've completed the TLSAE course and passed your vision test as described above, the next step is to take the written knowledge exam. This written portion of your driving test is conducted on a TouchScreen Terminal at the DMV and is offered in several languages.

To pass the Knowledge Exam, you need to answer 38 out of 46 questions correctly, or 83%. Otherwise, your application will be disqualified and you will have to apply again if you fail to pass it within the 12-month application period. You must wait 7 days before taking it again. Importantly, questions are multiple-choice with two wrong and one correct answer only.

4. Road test

The last step to receiving your California driver's license is a road test. This can be booked at any local DMV and lasts about 20 minutes. Bear in mind that you'll need to show your proof of insurance before undertaking the test. You'll also need to provide your vehicle, which must meet the following:

1. Functional windshield wipers, headlights, and seatbelts
2. Good visibility through all windows
3. A functioning horn, brakes, tires, steering wheels, turn signals, rear-view mirrors, and brake lights
4. A valid license plate
5. Adequate gas

You will also need to provide all of your documents for the California driving test. You may be required to execute the following instructions during the exam:

1. Staying in your lane
2. Maintaining proper speed
3. A quick stop from 20 mph
4. Signaling, turning, and passing
5. A three-point turn
6. Approaching an intersection
7. Observe right of way
8. Parking in standard conditions and on a hill
9. Moving in reverse for about 50 feet

The examiner will take note of your performance to make sure you're obeying traffic laws, such as all traffic signals, including stop signs. They'll also observe your following distance and the correctness of your posture. There is an additional retesting fee if you do not pass the first time.

Issuance of license

After passing the tests, you can provide your documents and pay the licensing fee for your California driver's license. In addition, a photograph of you is taken and your fingerprint scanned. The license correct for your status and age will then be issued to you.

https://driving-tests.org/california/drivers-license-guide/

Practice Test 1

Directions:

1.   There is no time limit.

2.   There are 46 multiple choice questions on this exam.

3.   **Phones and pagers are not allowed. Having either will result in automatic dismissal from the exam and nullification of exam scores.**

Tips:

- Answer all questions even if you are unsure.
- Mark any questions you are stuck on and revisit them after you are done. The exam is not timed so take your time.
- After reading the question, try answering it in your head first to avoid getting confused by the choices.
- Read the entire question before looking at the answers.
- Use the process of elimination to filter out choices that don't seem correct to increase your chances of selecting the correct answer.
- Be aware of important keywords like **not, sometimes, always,** and **never**. These words completely alter the ask of the question so it's important to keep track of them.

PLEASE READ THESE INSTRUCTIONS CAREFULLY.

Name: _____   Date: _____

1.	Ⓐ Ⓑ Ⓒ Ⓓ	24.	Ⓐ Ⓑ Ⓒ Ⓓ
2.	Ⓐ Ⓑ Ⓒ Ⓓ	25.	Ⓐ Ⓑ Ⓒ Ⓓ
3.	Ⓐ Ⓑ Ⓒ Ⓓ	26.	Ⓐ Ⓑ Ⓒ Ⓓ
4.	Ⓐ Ⓑ Ⓒ Ⓓ	27.	Ⓐ Ⓑ Ⓒ Ⓓ
5.	Ⓐ Ⓑ Ⓒ Ⓓ	28.	Ⓐ Ⓑ Ⓒ Ⓓ
6.	Ⓐ Ⓑ Ⓒ Ⓓ	29.	Ⓐ Ⓑ Ⓒ Ⓓ
7.	Ⓐ Ⓑ Ⓒ Ⓓ	30.	Ⓐ Ⓑ Ⓒ Ⓓ
8.	Ⓐ Ⓑ Ⓒ Ⓓ	31.	Ⓐ Ⓑ Ⓒ Ⓓ
9.	Ⓐ Ⓑ Ⓒ Ⓓ	32.	Ⓐ Ⓑ Ⓒ Ⓓ
10.	Ⓐ Ⓑ Ⓒ Ⓓ	33.	Ⓐ Ⓑ Ⓒ Ⓓ
11.	Ⓐ Ⓑ Ⓒ Ⓓ	34.	Ⓐ Ⓑ Ⓒ Ⓓ
12.	Ⓐ Ⓑ Ⓒ Ⓓ	35.	Ⓐ Ⓑ Ⓒ Ⓓ
13.	Ⓐ Ⓑ Ⓒ Ⓓ	36.	Ⓐ Ⓑ Ⓒ Ⓓ
14.	Ⓐ Ⓑ Ⓒ Ⓓ	37.	Ⓐ Ⓑ Ⓒ Ⓓ
15.	Ⓐ Ⓑ Ⓒ Ⓓ	38.	Ⓐ Ⓑ Ⓒ Ⓓ
16.	Ⓐ Ⓑ Ⓒ Ⓓ	39.	Ⓐ Ⓑ Ⓒ Ⓓ
17	Ⓐ Ⓑ Ⓒ Ⓓ	40.	Ⓐ Ⓑ Ⓒ Ⓓ
18.	Ⓐ Ⓑ Ⓒ Ⓓ	41.	Ⓐ Ⓑ Ⓒ Ⓓ
19.	Ⓐ Ⓑ Ⓒ Ⓓ	42.	Ⓐ Ⓑ Ⓒ Ⓓ
20.	Ⓐ Ⓑ Ⓒ Ⓓ	43.	Ⓐ Ⓑ Ⓒ Ⓓ
21.	Ⓐ Ⓑ Ⓒ Ⓓ	44.	Ⓐ Ⓑ Ⓒ Ⓓ
22.	Ⓐ Ⓑ Ⓒ Ⓓ	45.	Ⓐ Ⓑ Ⓒ Ⓓ
23.	Ⓐ Ⓑ Ⓒ Ⓓ	46.	Ⓐ Ⓑ Ⓒ Ⓓ

1. If eligible, you may renew your license by mail __ times in a row.

   A. 2
   B. 4
   C. 6
   D. 8

2. Heavy rain or snowfall may prevent you from seeing further than 100 feet. To maintain safety, drivers should not exceed __ mph.

   A. 30
   B. 20
   C. 80
   D. 10

3. The speed limit in a residential neighborhood is ___ unless otherwise indicated.

   A. 22 mph
   B. 25 mph
   C. 30 mph
   D. 10 mph

4. After signaling on a motorway, at least __ seconds must pass before changing lanes.

   A. 5
   B. 2
   C. 6
   D. 4

5. You may go off the paved road to pass another car:

A. At all times
B. Under no circumstances
C. If you signal beforehand
D. In an emergency

6. As you merge onto the freeway, you should be driving

A. At or near the same speed
B. At a different speed
C. At a slow speed
D. At a high speed

7. As you approach a railroad crossing, there are no visible warning signs and you cannot see 400 feet down the rails. The permitted speed is:

A. 15
B. 13
C. 12
D. 11

8. On a level street, your car must be parked parallel to the curb as follows:

A. 15 inches away from the curb
B. 13 inches away from the curb
C. 12 inches away from the curb
D. 18 inches away from the curb

9. When driving in foggy conditions, utilize your:

   A. High beams
   B. Low beams
   C. Normal beams
   D. Fog lights

10. Collisions may occur more frequently when:

   A. All cars are going above the posted speed limit
   B. All vehicles are traveling at about the same speed
   C. One vehicle is traveling faster or slower than all other vehicles
   D. Drivers signal before turning

11. A white colored curb means:

   A. No parking
   B. Ambulance only
   C. Trucks only
   D. Passengers or mail only

12. Why is driving at night more difficult than daytime driving?

   A. There is more traffic at night
   B. There are more drunk drivers at night
   C. There is reduced visibility at night
   D. There are no traffic signals at night

13. Highways are frequently the slickest:

    A. During a summer thunderstorm with heavy rain
    B. When it first starts to rain after a dry spell
    C. After it has been raining for a long time
    D. When there is an oil spillage present

14. In an emergency, you should:

    A. Think before you act
    B. Leave as soon as possible
    C. Follow your gut impulses
    D. Panic

15. The road is particularly slick when it starts to rain on a hot day:

    A. For the first few minutes
    B. A few hours after heavy rainfall
    C. After it has stopped raining
    D. No, it happens during winters

16. Most crashes occurring in a work zone:

    A. Occur at night
    B. Are minor in nature
    C. Are rear–end collisions
    D. Occur during the day

17. According to state law, what must you do if there are injuries or property damages totaling more than $750 in an accident?

    A. Submit a Report of Traffic Accident Occurring in California to the DMV within 10 days
    B. File a report with the IRS
    C. File a report with the police only
    D. Run away from the scene

18. What should you do if you lightly collide with an unoccupied parked car?

    A. Leave a note on the vehicle to let the owner know about the incident
    B. Report the accident immediately to local police
    C. Both A & B
    D. None of the above

19. If the other driver is injured during a collision, the first thing you should do is:

    A. Give aid to the injured driver, but do not move him/her
    B. Call the police
    C. Call your lawyer
    D. Call your insurance company

20. Which of these statements is true about motorcycles?

    A. Motorcycles are small and can easily be seen by drivers
    B. Motorcycles may not share traffic lanes
    C. Motorcycles should be followed at a 4 second following distance
    D. Motorcycles are faster than cars

21. Which of the following statements is accurate regarding safety belts and collisions?

    A. They are not necessary if your car has front and side airbags

    B. They keep you from being thrown clear to safety, which lowers your chances of surviving collisions

    C. They increase your chances of survival in most types of collisions

    D. They are optional when driving slowly

22. A police car behind you urges you to stop. You veer off course, striking another vehicle and injuring an individual. You are liable for:

    A. Imprisonment in a state prison for up to seven years

    B. A fine of not less than $1000

    C. Attending an anger management class

    D. Paying two months of the individual's foregone income due to injury

23. When trying to avoid a rear-end collision, you should:

    A. Signal at least 100 feet before turning

    B. Decrease your following distance

    C. Quickly pump your brakes just before turning

    D. Pull up the hand brake

24. In the state of California, you must report a traffic accident to the DMV when:

    A. Your vehicle fails a smog test

    B. You are involved in a collision and there is an injury

    C. You change your insurance company

    D. You see someone fleeing

25. Why should you not tailgate other drivers?

   A. It is illegal to do so
   B. Other drivers might tailgate you in return
   C. You risk making the other drivers angry and frustrated
   D. You will face a collision

26. Alcohol will:

   A. Impair your judgement and reduce your reaction time
   B. Reduce your ability to recover from glare
   C. Blur your vision
   D. All of the above

27. After drinking alcohol, you should:

   A. Drive home yourself
   B. Drive home with a friend
   C. Take a cab home
   D. Ride a motorcycle home

28. Alcohol is a(n)

   A. Antioxidant
   B. Stimulus
   C. Depressant
   D. Drug

29. How long does it take your body to process three beers?

    A. 1 hour
    B. 3 hours
    C. 4 hours
    D. 6 hours

30. Which of the following situations would not require you to keep your wheels pointed forward?

    A. When waiting to make a left turn at a traffic light
    B. When parked on a hill or sloping driveway
    C. When left parked along the side of an open, flat road without a curb
    D. While driving

31. How many alcoholic beverages does it take to affect your driving?

    A. 1 drink
    B. 2 drinks
    C. 3 drinks
    D. 4 drinks

32. When driving in rain, snow, or fog you should use

    A. Low beams
    B. High beams
    C. Fog lights only
    D. Headlights

33. This sign means:

A. You are approaching a railroad crossing and should prepare to stop
B. Always stop at the upcoming railroad crossing
C. Should stop and wait for a signal before crossing the railroad tracks
D. Wait for the traffic police to signal when it's okay to cross

34. What angle should your hands be in relation to the steering wheel?

A. 12 O'clock and 6 O'clock
B. 2 O'clock and 3 O'clock
C. 9 O'clock and 3 O'clock
D. 5 O'clock and 7 O'clock

35. When you need to make a right turn and a truck or bus is also making a right turn, you should:

A. Quickly turn before the truck or bus can
B. Wait until the truck or bus turns before you turn
C. Squeeze between the truck or bus and the curb
D. Speed up because you have the right of way

36. When travelling on ice or snowy roads:

A. It is safe to use your cruise control
B. Make speed and directional changes more gradually than you would otherwise
C. Drive as you would under normal conditions
D. You should turn on low beams

37. When the yellow centerline is broken, it means:

    A. Passing is not permitted
    B. Passing on the right is permitted when the way ahead is clear
    C. Passing on the left is permitted when the way ahead is clear
    D. You cannot pass

38. Countdown traffic signal lights:

    A. Indicate how many seconds remain for crossing
    B. Indicate nothing
    C. Indicate how much time is left before reaching home
    D. Indicate how fast you can drive

39. Which of the following is true regarding lane changes?

    A. You only need to turn and look over your right shoulder for lane changes to the right or left
    B. Look over your right shoulder for a right lane change and your left shoulder for a left lane change
    C. Vehicles with two outside mirrors do not have blind spots
    D. You are not allowed to change lanes ever

40. You may drive in a bike lane:

    A. If you drive slower than 15 mph
    B. No more than 200 feet before making a right turn
    C. Whenever bicyclists are not present
    D. If you drive faster than 20 mph

41. This sign means:

A. You should drive faster
B. You must slow down to 10 mph
C. You must make a full stop
D. You should drive slowly if there are pedestrians

42. You must be able to clearly see at least _____ feet ahead of you before passing on the left.

A. 100
B. 200
C. 400
D. 150

43. How far ahead should you scan the road for potential dangers?

A. 3 feet
B. 2 feet
C. 1 foot
D. 7 feet

44. What is the maximum allowed speed in business districts?

A. 25 mph
B. 10 mph
C. 12 mph
D. 13 mph

45. In the middle of the road, there are two sets of solid double yellow lines that are separated by at least two feet. These are regarded as:

    A. A sign that an expressway is ahead
    B. A barrier that you may not pass for any reason
    C. A lane that you may pass freely
    D. A crossway

46. At what speed can your tires hydroplane on slick roadways during a downpour?

    A. 10 mph
    B. 50 mph
    C. 12 mph
    D. 9 mph

Answer Key

.   A. 2

.   A. 30

.   B. 25 mph

.   A. 5

.   B. Under no circumstances

.   A. At or near the same speed

.   A. 15

.   D. 18 inches away from the curb

.   B. Low beams

0.   C. One vehicle is traveling faster or slower than all other vehicles

1.   D. Passengers or mail only

2.   C. There is reduced visibility at night

3.   B. When it first starts to rain after a dry spell

4.   A. Think before you act

5.   A. For the first few minutes

6.   C. Are rear–end collisions

7.   A. Submit a Report of Traffic Accident Occurring in California to the DMV within 10 days

8.   C. Both A & B

9.   A. Give aid to the injured driver, but do not move him/her

0.   C. Motorcycles should be followed at a 4 second following distance

1.   C. They increase your chances of survival in most types of collisions

22.   A. Imprisonment in a state prison for up to seven years

23.   A. Signaling at least 100 feet before turning

24.   B. You are involved in a collision and there is an injury

25.   C. You risk making the other drivers angry and frustrated

26.   D. All of the above

27.   C. Take a cab home

28.   C. Depressant

29.   B. 3 hours

30.   B. When parked on a hill or sloping driveway

31.   A. 1 drink

32.   A. Low beams

33.   A. You are approaching a railroad crossing and should prepare to stop

34.   C. 9 O'clock and 3 O'clock

35.   B. Wait until the truck or bus turns before you turn

36.   B. Make speed and directional changes more gradually than you would otherwise

37.   C. Passing on the left is permitted when the way ahead is clear

38.   A. Indicate how many seconds remain for crossing

39.   B. Look over your right shoulder for a right lane change and your left shoulder for a left lane change

40.   B. No more than 200 feet before making a right turn

41.   C. You must make a full stop

42.   C. 400

43.   A. 3 feet

44.   A. 25 mph

45.   B. A barrier-you may not enter for any reason

46.   B. 50 mph

Practice Test 2

Directions:

1.	There is no time limit.

2.	There are 46 multiple choice questions on this exam.

3.	**Phones and pagers are not allowed. Having either will result in automatic dismissal from the exam and nullification of exam scores.**

Tips:

- Answer all questions even if you are unsure.
- Mark any questions you are stuck on and revisit them after you are done. The exam is timed so make sure you finish as many questions as you can.
- After reading the question, try answering it in your head first to avoid getting confused by the choices.
- Read the entire question before looking at the answers.
- Use the process of elimination to filter out choices that don't seem correct to increase your chances of selecting the correct answer.
- Be aware of important keywords like **not, sometimes, always,** and **never**. These words completely alter the ask of the question so it's important to keep track of them.

PLEASE READ THESE INSTRUCTIONS CAREFULLY.

Name: _____   Date: _____

1.	Ⓐ Ⓑ Ⓒ Ⓓ	24.	Ⓐ Ⓑ Ⓒ Ⓓ
2.	Ⓐ Ⓑ Ⓒ Ⓓ	25.	Ⓐ Ⓑ Ⓒ Ⓓ
3.	Ⓐ Ⓑ Ⓒ Ⓓ	26.	Ⓐ Ⓑ Ⓒ Ⓓ
4.	Ⓐ Ⓑ Ⓒ Ⓓ	27.	Ⓐ Ⓑ Ⓒ Ⓓ
5.	Ⓐ Ⓑ Ⓒ Ⓓ	28.	Ⓐ Ⓑ Ⓒ Ⓓ
6.	Ⓐ Ⓑ Ⓒ Ⓓ	29.	Ⓐ Ⓑ Ⓒ Ⓓ
7.	Ⓐ Ⓑ Ⓒ Ⓓ	30.	Ⓐ Ⓑ Ⓒ Ⓓ
8.	Ⓐ Ⓑ Ⓒ Ⓓ	31.	Ⓐ Ⓑ Ⓒ Ⓓ
9.	Ⓐ Ⓑ Ⓒ Ⓓ	32.	Ⓐ Ⓑ Ⓒ Ⓓ
10.	Ⓐ Ⓑ Ⓒ Ⓓ	33.	Ⓐ Ⓑ Ⓒ Ⓓ
11.	Ⓐ Ⓑ Ⓒ Ⓓ	34.	Ⓐ Ⓑ Ⓒ Ⓓ
12.	Ⓐ Ⓑ Ⓒ Ⓓ	35.	Ⓐ Ⓑ Ⓒ Ⓓ
13.	Ⓐ Ⓑ Ⓒ Ⓓ	36.	Ⓐ Ⓑ Ⓒ Ⓓ
14.	Ⓐ Ⓑ Ⓒ Ⓓ	37.	Ⓐ Ⓑ Ⓒ Ⓓ
15.	Ⓐ Ⓑ Ⓒ Ⓓ	38.	Ⓐ Ⓑ Ⓒ Ⓓ
16.	Ⓐ Ⓑ Ⓒ Ⓓ	39.	Ⓐ Ⓑ Ⓒ Ⓓ
17	Ⓐ Ⓑ Ⓒ Ⓓ	40.	Ⓐ Ⓑ Ⓒ Ⓓ
18.	Ⓐ Ⓑ Ⓒ Ⓓ	41.	Ⓐ Ⓑ Ⓒ Ⓓ
19.	Ⓐ Ⓑ Ⓒ Ⓓ	42.	Ⓐ Ⓑ Ⓒ Ⓓ
20.	Ⓐ Ⓑ Ⓒ Ⓓ	43.	Ⓐ Ⓑ Ⓒ Ⓓ
21.	Ⓐ Ⓑ Ⓒ Ⓓ	44.	Ⓐ Ⓑ Ⓒ Ⓓ
22.	Ⓐ Ⓑ Ⓒ Ⓓ	45.	Ⓐ Ⓑ Ⓒ Ⓓ
23.	Ⓐ Ⓑ Ⓒ Ⓓ	46.	Ⓐ Ⓑ Ⓒ Ⓓ

1. When following another vehicle, you must turn your lights down within _____ feet.

   A. 200
   B. 300
   C. 120
   D. 400

2. Statistically, about one in every ___ American will be involved in a crash that was caused by alcohol.

   A. 2
   B. 4
   C. 5
   D. 3

3. Approximately one in ten drivers_____.

   A. Die
   B. Live
   C. Are involved in a crash every year
   D. Are involved in a collision every two years

4. If you buy a car from a private seller, you have __ days to transfer the title.

   A. 10
   B. 5
   C. 6
   D. 7

5. A school bus with red flashing lights is stopped in your lane up ahead. You should:

   A. Continue driving
   B. Stop when the red lights are flashing
   C. Drive fast
   D. Drive slowly

6. How fast should you go through a blind intersection?

   A. 10 mph
   B. 12 mph
   C. 13 mph
   D. 15 mph

7. If the percentage of alcohol in your blood is ____, you are considered intoxicated.

   A. 0.07%
   B. 0.08%
   C. 0.09%
   D. 0.10%

8. You are preparing for a left turn. You must consistently signal _____ prior to actually turning

   A. 50 feet
   B. 100 feet
   C. 20 feet
   D. 10 feet

9. What should you turn on if you are driving in a dust storm to aid with the reduced visibility?

A. Headlights
B. Signal
C. Emergency lights
D. Fog Lamps

10. If you are found guilty of operating a vehicle while intoxicated, you could receive the following sentence:

A. Up to six months in jail
B. Up to two months in jail
C. No jail time but you must pay a fine of $500
D. Up to 1 year

11. When parking on a two-way street that has no curb, your wheels should be:

A. Perpendicular
B. Straight
C. Turned toward the street
D. Turned away from the street

12. If you're over 21 and have never been arrested for DUI and are suspected of operating under the influence, what will happen if you refuse a chemical test?

A. Your license will be suspended for 1 year
B. Your license will be suspended for 180 days
C. You will be fined $1000
D. Nothing will happen

13. A BAC (blood alcohol content) of _____ or above is prohibited if you are over 21.

    A.   0.01
    B.   0.04
    C.   0.08
    D.   0.06

14. Consistently signaling in the final 100 feet before making a turn is a good habit:

    A.   Unless you are in designated turn lane
    B.   Unless your turn is protected by a green arrow
    C.   Even if you do not see other vehicles around
    D.   Unless your turn is protected by a red arrow

15. Anyone who operates a motor vehicle in California has given agreement to submit to a chemical test to determine the amount of alcohol in their blood, breath, or urine.

    A.   If asked by law enforcement
    B.   Only if you have been drinking alcohol
    C.   Only if a collision has occurred
    D.   Only if you drive fast

16. At an approaching intersection, a flashing yellow traffic light is visible. The flashing light means:

    A.   Drive fast
    B.   Cross intersection fast
    C.   Drive slowly
    D.   Slow down and cross the intersection carefully

17. 12 ounces of beer will typically leave your system in about:

    A. 1/2 hour
    B. 1 hour
    C. 2 hours
    D. 4 hours

18. What does a chemical test assess?

    A. Blood alcohol content
    B. Fatigue level
    C. Vision
    D. Eyesight

19. Prescription or over the counter drugs can:

    A   Enhance your senses
    B. Multiply the effect of alcohol
    C. Wake you up
    D. Improve your vision

20. Drinking coffee after you drink alcohol can:

    A. Improve your reaction time
    B. Increase your alertness
    C. Cancels the effect of alcohol
    D. None of the above

21. After drinking, what is the only accurate method to get sober enough to drive?

    A.   Wait 3 hours for your body to process the alcohol
    B.   Drink tea before you drive
    C.   Drink lots of water before you drive
    D.   Drink hard liquor to cleanse the body

22. When you have both alcohol and drugs in your blood:

    A.   The effects of both increase
    B.   The effects of the drugs increase
    C.   The effects of alcohol increase
    D.   The effect decreases

23. What should you do before operating a motor vehicle if you are taking non-prescription medicine?

    A.   Drink lots of water
    B.   Check the label for warnings
    C.   Wait 3 hours before you drive after taking the drug
    D.   Sit down

24. You have agreed to the following when driving in the United States:

    A.   You are over the age of 21
    B.   You have no criminal record
    C.   You agree to test the alcohol level in your blood, breath, and urine
    D.   You swear to tell the truth and nothing but the truth

25. Which of the following can have an impact on your driving?

    A. Alcohol and marijuana
    B. Cough syrups and cold tablets
    C. Anesthesia
    D. All of the above

26. Which of the following claims about drug use and driving is accurate?

    A. Any prescription drug is safe to use if you do not feel drowsy
    B. Even over–the–counter drugs can impair your driving
    C. Only illegal drugs can impair your driving
    D. Nothing can impair your driving

27. Which of the following factors doesn't affect blood alcohol content (BAC)?

    A. How fit you are
    B. Your body weight
    C. How much time has passed since you drank
    D. How tall you are

28. Whose duty is it to understand how drugs affect your ability to drive?

    A. Your pharmacist's
    B. Your physician's
    C. Yours
    D. Your parents'

29. If you are under 21 years old, you may be subject to administrative punishment if your BAC (blood alcohol content) is _____ or higher.

    A. 0.01
    B. 0.02
    C. 0.03
    D. 0.04

30. When being pursued by a tailgater, which of the following will prevent you from getting struck from behind?

    A. Merging into another lane
    B. Decreasing your following distance
    C. Changing lanes frequently
    D. Doing nothing

31. This sign means:

    A. Approaching traffic must stop at the intersection
    B. Be prepared to stop, slow down, and look both ways for trains
    C. Do not enter
    D. The street ahead is a school zone

32. As you approach a traffic light with a red signal. a police officer instructs you to proceed through the intersection without stopping. You should:

    A. Stop until the light turns green
    B. Go through the intersection without stopping
    C. Come to a complete stop before proceeding
    D. Get out the car and drop to your knees

33. Which of the following factors influence how well someone absorbs alcohol?

A. Weight
B. Height
C. Intelligence
D. Face

34. A red and orange triangle shaped sign means:

A. The vehicle has the right-of-way
B. Slow-moving vehicle
C. Shoulder work ahead
D. Stop

35.

SLOWER
TRAFFIC
KEEP
RIGHT

This sign means:

A. You should slow down and move to the right lane
B. Stay in the right lane if you are driving more slowly than other traffic
C. Slower traffic must exit on the right
D. You should drive faster

36. Fatigue increases the risk of:

A. Missing an exit
B. Being late for an appointment
C. Falling asleep behind the wheel and crashing
D. Agitation

37.

This sign means:

A. Cars on the right move first
B. You have the right-of-way
C. Let cross traffic pass before proceeding
D. Stop

38. In the majority of cases, how many passengers must be present in a vehicle to lawfully use the carpool lane?

A. 2 people
B. 3 people
C. 1 person
D. 8 people

39. Which of the following blocks the smooth flow of traffic?

A. Slowing down to look at collision scene
B. Avoiding unnecessary lane changes
C. Using public transportation instead of your vehicle
D. Driving at the speed limit on a highway

40. School zone speed limit:

A. 35 miles per hour
B. 30 miles per hour
C. 25 miles per hour
D. 10 miles per hour

41. Blind intersection speed limit:

    A. 10 mph
    B. 15 mph
    C. 13 mph
    D. 40 mph

42. You are on a road with only one lane in each direction and you want to pass another vehicle, but there is a curve ahead which blocks your view. You must:

    A. Not pass the other vehicle
    B. Pass on the shoulder of the road
    C. Signal longer than five seconds to pass safely
    D. Stop the car

43. More ___of licensed teen drivers have a vehicle crash before age twenty.

    A. 30%
    B. 40%
    C. 50%
    D. None of the above

44. Running a red light at an intersection will result in _____ being added to your driving record.

    A. 2 points
    B. 7 points
    C. 3 points
    D. 4 points.

45. It is dark, and the high lights from a car approaching make it difficult to see the road in front of you. You should:

    A. Look ahead towards the left edge of your lane
    B. Look ahead towards the right edge of your lane
    C. Look straight ahead in your lane
    D. Look at the center

46. You may drive in a bike lane:

    A. No more than 200 feet before making a right turn
    B. Never
    C. Always
    D. No more than 500 feet before making a right turn

Answer Key

1.   B. 300

2.   D. 3

3.   C. Are involved in a crash every year

4.   A. 10

5.   B. Stop when the red lights are flashing

6.   D. 15 mph

7.   B. 0.08%

8.   B. 100 feet

9.   A. Headlights

10.   A. Up to six months in jail

11.   D. Turned away from the street

12.   B. Your license will be suspended for 180 days

13.   C. 0.08

14.   C. Even if you do not see other vehicles around

15.   A. If asked by law enforcement

16.   D. Slow down and cross the intersection carefully

17.   B. 1 hour

18.   A. Blood alcohol content

19.   B. Multiply the effect of alcohol

20.   D. None of the above

21.   A. Wait 3 hours for your body to process the alcohol

22.   A. The effects of both increase

23.   B. Check the label for warnings

24.   C. You agree to test for the alcohol level in your blood, breath, or urine

25.   D. All of the above

26.   B. Even over–the–counter drugs can impair your driving

27.   A. How fit you are

28.   C. Yours

29.   A. 0.01

30.   A. Merging into another lane

31.   A. Approaching traffic must stop at the intersection

32.   B. Go through the intersection without stopping

33.   A. Weight

34.   B. Slow-moving vehicle

35.   B. Stay in the right lane if you are driving more slowly than other traffic

36.   C. Falling asleep behind the wheel and crashing

37.   C. Let cross traffic pass before proceeding

38.   A. 2 people

39.   A. Slowing down to look at collision scene

40.   C. 25 miles per hour

41.   B. 15 mph

42.   A. Not pass the other vehicle

43.   C. 50%

44.   C. 3 points

45.   B. Look ahead towards the right edge of your lane

46.   A. No more than 200 feet before making a right turn

43

Practice Test 3

Directions:

1. There is no time limit.

2. There are 46 multiple choice questions on this exam.

3. **Phones and pagers are not allowed. Having either will result in automatic dismissal from the exam and nullification of exam scores.**

Tips:

- Answer all questions even if you are unsure.
- Mark any questions you are stuck on and revisit them after you are done. The exam is timed so make sure you finish as many questions as you can.
- After reading the question, try answering it in your head first to avoid getting confused by the choices.
- Read the entire question before looking at the answers.
- Use the process of elimination to filter out choices that don't seem correct to increase your chances of selecting the correct answer.
- Be aware of important keywords like **not, sometimes, always,** and **never**. These words completely alter the ask of the question so it's important to keep track of them.

PLEASE READ THESE INSTRUCTIONS CAREFULLY.

Name: _____   Date: _____

1.	Ⓐ Ⓑ Ⓒ Ⓓ			24.	Ⓐ Ⓑ Ⓒ Ⓓ
2.	Ⓐ Ⓑ Ⓒ Ⓓ			25.	Ⓐ Ⓑ Ⓒ Ⓓ
3.	Ⓐ Ⓑ Ⓒ Ⓓ			26.	Ⓐ Ⓑ Ⓒ Ⓓ
4.	Ⓐ Ⓑ Ⓒ Ⓓ			27.	Ⓐ Ⓑ Ⓒ Ⓓ
5.	Ⓐ Ⓑ Ⓒ Ⓓ			28.	Ⓐ Ⓑ Ⓒ Ⓓ
6.	Ⓐ Ⓑ Ⓒ Ⓓ			29.	Ⓐ Ⓑ Ⓒ Ⓓ
7.	Ⓐ Ⓑ Ⓒ Ⓓ			30.	Ⓐ Ⓑ Ⓒ Ⓓ
8.	Ⓐ Ⓑ Ⓒ Ⓓ			31.	Ⓐ Ⓑ Ⓒ Ⓓ
9.	Ⓐ Ⓑ Ⓒ Ⓓ			32.	Ⓐ Ⓑ Ⓒ Ⓓ
10.	Ⓐ Ⓑ Ⓒ Ⓓ			33.	Ⓐ Ⓑ Ⓒ Ⓓ
11.	Ⓐ Ⓑ Ⓒ Ⓓ			34.	Ⓐ Ⓑ Ⓒ Ⓓ
12.	Ⓐ Ⓑ Ⓒ Ⓓ			35.	Ⓐ Ⓑ Ⓒ Ⓓ
13.	Ⓐ Ⓑ Ⓒ Ⓓ			36.	Ⓐ Ⓑ Ⓒ Ⓓ
14.	Ⓐ Ⓑ Ⓒ Ⓓ			37.	Ⓐ Ⓑ Ⓒ Ⓓ
15.	Ⓐ Ⓑ Ⓒ Ⓓ			38.	Ⓐ Ⓑ Ⓒ Ⓓ
16.	Ⓐ Ⓑ Ⓒ Ⓓ			39.	Ⓐ Ⓑ Ⓒ Ⓓ
17	Ⓐ Ⓑ Ⓒ Ⓓ			40.	Ⓐ Ⓑ Ⓒ Ⓓ
18.	Ⓐ Ⓑ Ⓒ Ⓓ			41.	Ⓐ Ⓑ Ⓒ Ⓓ
19.	Ⓐ Ⓑ Ⓒ Ⓓ			42.	Ⓐ Ⓑ Ⓒ Ⓓ
20.	Ⓐ Ⓑ Ⓒ Ⓓ			43.	Ⓐ Ⓑ Ⓒ Ⓓ
21.	Ⓐ Ⓑ Ⓒ Ⓓ			44.	Ⓐ Ⓑ Ⓒ Ⓓ
22.	Ⓐ Ⓑ Ⓒ Ⓓ			45.	Ⓐ Ⓑ Ⓒ Ⓓ
23.	Ⓐ Ⓑ Ⓒ Ⓓ			46.	Ⓐ Ⓑ Ⓒ Ⓓ

                                       Practice Test

1. Which gear should you use if you want to back up?

   A. Drive
   B. Reverse
   C. Neutral
   D. Park

2. The duration of a driver's license in California is ___ years.

   A. 6
   B. 5
   C. 8
   D. 11

3. You must inform the DMV of any car transfers or sales within __ days.

   A. 5
   B. 8
   C. 9
   D. 7

4. To _____, a non-commercial Class B license is necessary.

   A. Drive a truck
   B. Ride a boat
   C. Fly a plane
   D. Drive a 40–foot motor home

5. A person who holds a Class C driver's license is permitted to:

    A. Drive a truck
    B Ride a motorcycle
    C. Drive a 2 decker bus
    D. A 3–axle vehicle if the gross vehicle weight is less than 6,000 pounds

6. When driving down a steep hill, which gear should you use?

    A. Low
    B. Middle
    C. High
    D. None of the above

7. If you are turning left from a multilane one-way street onto a one-way street, you should begin your turn:

    A. The lane closest to the left curb
    B. From nowhere
    C. From behind
    D. The lane to the right of the curb

8. You want to make a right turn at an upcoming intersection. You should slow down and:

    A. Do nothing
    B. Signal for 100 feet before turning
    C. Signal for 50 feet before turning
    D. Reverse

9. You are travelling at 65 mph on a freeway but traffic is moving 70 mph. You are allowed to drive:

   A. Slower than 50 mph
   B. Faster than 70 mph
   C. At 70 mph
   D. No faster than 65 mph

10. What should you do if you are waiting to make a left turn at an intersection?

    A. Signal and make sure your wheels are turned to the right
    B. Signal and make sure your wheels are turned to the left
    C. Signal and keep your wheels straight
    D. Signal and do nothing

11. It is illegal to park your vehicle:

    A. In front of your house
    B. In an unmarked crosswalk
    C. In front of a hospital
    D. In front of a lake

12. You must stop when you come to a crossing where a blind pedestrian is waiting to cross:

    A. More than five feet from the crosswalk so the pedestrian will not be distracted by the sound of your engine
    B. At the crosswalk and wait for the pedestrian to cross the street
    C. At the crosswalk and then tell the pedestrian when to cross the street
    D. You should not stop

13. When is it permitted to legally block an intersection?

    A.   You cannot legally block an intersection

    B.   During rush hours

    C.   During a traffic jam

    D.   When you cross a yellow light right before it turns red

14. Who has the right–of–way at an intersection with no crosswalks?

    A.   Pedestrians always have the right–of–way

    B.   Vehicles, but they should slow down and be careful

    C.   Pedestrians, but only with the green walk signal

    D.   No one

15. When two vehicles arrive at an all-way stop intersection at the same time, which vehicle can go first?

    A.   The vehicle on the left

    B.   The vehicle on the right

    C.   The newer vehicle

    D.   The vehicle on the center

16. As you are crossing on intersection, an emergency vehicle is approaching with a siren and flashing lights. You should:

    A.   Stop immediately in the intersection until it passes

    B.   Pull to the right in the intersection and stop

    C.   Continue through the intersection, pull to the right, and stop

    D.   Continue driving normally

17. If the rear end of your cars starts skidding to the left, you should:

    A. Steer to the right
    B. Steer to the left
    C. Brake hard
    D. Steer straight

18. When you are unable to stop safely at a yellow traffic light, you should:

    A. Stop your vehicle before entering the intersection anyway
    B. Enter the intersection cautiously and continue across
    C. Stop your vehicle in the intersection and back up carefully
    D. Drive faster

19. You are waiting to turn right at a red traffic light. There is a pedestrian on the right side of your vehicle waiting to cross the street you want to enter. Who has the right–of–way when your light turns green?

    A. The pedestrian has the right–of–way
    B. You have the right–of–way only if the crosswalk is not marked
    C. You have the right–of–way because your light is green
    D. No one has the right

20. You must yield to a pedestrian using a white cane or guide dog:

    A. Only when the guide dog is leading the person across a street
    B. Only when the pedestrian is obeying traffic controls
    C. At all times
    D. Only when the pedestrian has a yellow badge

21. If you know you will block an intersection when the light turns red, you should not begin crossing an intersection:

    A. Under any circumstances
    B. Unless you entered the intersection on a yellow light
    C. Unless you entered the intersection on a green light
    D. Unless there are no cars around

22. After passing a car, you should return to the right lane when:

    A. There is no car in the right lane
    B. There is no car ahead of you
    C. You can see the front bumper of the other car in your mirror
    D. You cannot see the car

23. You want to make a right turn at the corner. A pedestrian with a guide dog is at the corner ready to cross the street in front of you. Before making your right turn, you should:

    A. Turn off your engine until the person crosses the street
    B. Tell the pedestrian when to cross the street
    C. Wait until the person crosses the street
    D. Honk lightly to get their attention

24. You should _____ when you are driving behind a large truck on the freeway?

    A. Honk three times
    B. Stay farther behind the truck than you normally would
    C. Drive normally
    D. Flash your headlights

25. To make a right turn onto a two–way street, start in the right–hand lane and end in:

    A. The left lane
    B. The lane closest to the curb
    C. Any land that is available
    D. To right lane

26. A pair of solid double yellow lines separated by spaces of at least two feet:

    A. May only be crossed to make a left turn or U–turn
    B. Should be treated like a solid wall and not be crossed
    C. May be used to begin or end left–hand turn
    D. May be crossed freely

27. To pass a bicyclist, you should:

    A. Move as far as possible to the right side of your lane
    B. Move as far as possible to the left side of your lane
    C. Speed up
    D. Stop

28. What does a solid yellow line next to a broken yellow line mean?

    A. Vehicles next to the broken line may pass
    B. Vehicles next to the solid line may pass
    C. Vehicles on both sides may pass
    D. No one can pass

29. What should you do if you are being tailgated?

    A.   Change into the right lane and let the vehicle from behind you pass

    B.   Speed up

    C.   Slow down to block the vehicle behind you

    D.   Get out of the car and confront the other driver

30. At the next intersection, you want to turn right. Slow down and perform the following:

    A.   Move toward the left side of your lane

    B.   Avoid driving in the bicycle lane

    C.   Signal 100 feet before turning

    D.   Signal 50 feet and turn

31. What should you do if you plan to pass another vehicle?

    A.   Assume the other driver will let you pass as long as you signal

    B.   Assume there is nothing at your blind spot without doing a shoulder check

    C.   Not assume the other driver will make space for you to pass

    D.   Come to a complete stop and signal, before finally turning

32. When driving in work zones, you should:

    A.   Increase your speed to get through the zone as quickly as possible

    B.   Reduce your speed and be prepared to stop suddenly

    C.   Maintain your normal speed the whole way through the zone

    D.   Come to a complete stop

33. When backing up, you should:

    A. Look through the rear window
    B. Press hard on the gas pedal
    C. Rely only on your rearview mirror
    D. Look out of your left window

35. You are driving the legal limit as you approach an intersection. The signal turns yellow, you should:

    A. Slow down and proceed through the intersection without caution
    B. Speed up to cross the intersection before the light turns red
    C. Stop before entering the intersection if you can do so safely
    D. Come to a screeching halt no matter what

34. A person may legally ride in the back of a pickup truck when:

    A. The sides of the pickup bed are at least 24 inches high
    B. The back of the pickup is covered with a camper shell
    C. In a secured seat and while using an approved safety belt
    D. Never

36. Which of these statements is true about drugs and driving?

    A. Any prescription drug is safe to use if you do not feel drowsy
    B. Even over-the-counter drugs can impair your driving
    C. Only illegal drugs can impair your driving
    D. There is no harm in it

37. When you are behind a motorcycle, you should:

   A. Be ready to use your horn
   B. Drive more slowly
   C. Allow a larger following distance
   D. Drive fast

38. You must notify the DMV within 5 days if you:

   A. Buy a car
   B. Sell or transfer your vehicle
   C. Crash your car
   D. Steal a car

39. When driving at night on a roadway with poor lighting, you should:

   A. Drive slow enough that you can stop within the area illuminated by your headlights
   B. Honk every few seconds because the sound will alert other drivers that you are near
   C. Keep the instrument panel lights bright to be more visible to other drivers
   D. Drive faster

40. California's "basic speed law" says you:

   A. Must never exceed 90 mph regardless of the area
   B. May only drive up to 30 mph in residential areas
   C. Always drive at least 30 mph on the freeway
   D. May never drive faster than is safe for current conditions

41. When are you legally allowed to block an intersection?

    A. Always
    B. Once a time
    C. Under no circumstances
    D. Twice

42. Sharing a lane with a motorcycle, known as _____, is illegal in California.

    A. Common lanes
    B. Lane sharing
    C. Lane splitting
    D. Road freedom

43. You're traveling at 55 mph on the highway and need to brake very suddenly. About how long will it take your car to come to a complete stop?

    A. 400 feet
    B. 200 feet
    C. 100 feet
    D. 50 feet

44. If a tow truck or emergency vehicle is stopped in your lane, you should:

    A. Slow down and when safe, move over a lane
    B. Switch lanes immediately
    C. Stop and wait until the vehicle moves
    D. Pull over and call the police

45. If a bus, trolley, or streetcar is stopped at a junction with a traffic signal, you must slow down so that you are not travelling any faster than:

    A. 5 mph
    B. 15 mph
    C. 12 mph
    D. 10 mph

46. You are on a two–way street with two lanes in each direction. To turn left, start the turn in:

    A. Any lane open to you for traffic in your direction
    B. The left lane for traffic in your direction
    C. The right lane for traffic in your direction
    D. The lane in the center

Answer Key

1. B. Reverse

2. B. 5

3. A. 5

4. D. Drive a 40–foot motor home

5. D. A 3–axle vehicle if the gross vehicle weight is less than 6,000 pounds

6. A. Low

7. A. The lane closest to the left curb

8. B. Signal for 100 feet before turning

9. D. No faster than 65 mph

10. C. Signal and keep your wheels straight

11. B. In an unmarked crosswalk

12. B. At the crosswalk and wait for the pedestrian to cross the street

13. A. You cannot legally block an intersection

14. A. Pedestrians always have the right–of–way

15. B. The vehicle on the right

16. C. Continue through the intersection, pull to the right, and stop

17. B. Steer to the left

18. B. Enter the intersection cautiously and continue across

19. A. The pedestrian has the right–of–way

20. C. At all times

21. A. Under any circumstances

22.   C. You can see the front bumper of the other car in your mirror

23.   C. Wait until the person crosses the street

24.   B. Stay farther behind the truck than you normally would

25.   B. The lane closest to the curb

26.   B. Should be treated like a solid wall and not be crossed

27.   B. Move as far as possible to the left side of your lane

28.   A. Vehicles next to the broken line may pass

29.   A. Change into the right lane and let the vehicle from behind you pass

30.   C. Signal for 100 feet before turning

31.   C. Not assume the other driver will make space for you to pass

32.   B. Reduce your speed and be prepared to stop suddenly

33.   A. Look through the rear window

34.   C. In a secured seat and while using an approved safety belt

35.   C. Stop before entering the intersection if you can do so safely

36.   B. Even over-the-counter drugs can impair your driving

37.   C. Allow a larger following distance

38.   B. Sell or transfer your vehicle

39.   A. Drive slowly enough that you can stop within the area illuminated by your headlights

40.   D. May never drive faster than is safe for current conditions

41.   C. Under no circumstances once so ever

42.   C. Lane splitting

43.   A. 400 feet

44.   A. Slow down and, if possible and safe, move over a lane

       Practice Test

45.   D. 10 mph

46.   B. The left lane for traffic in your direction

Practice Test 4

Directions:

1.   There is no time limit.

2.   There are 46 multiple choice questions on this exam.

3.   **Phones and pagers are not allowed. Having either will result in automatic dismissal from the exam and nullification of exam scores.**

Tips:

- Answer all questions even if you are unsure.
- Mark any questions you are stuck on and revisit them after you are done. The exam is timed so make sure you finish as many questions as you can.
- After reading the question, try answering it in your head first to avoid getting confused by the choices.
- Read the entire question before looking at the answers.
- Use the process of elimination to filter out choices that don't seem correct to increase your chances of selecting the correct answer.
- Be aware of important keywords like **not, sometimes, always,** and **never**. These words completely alter the ask of the question so it's important to keep track of them.

PLEASE READ THESE INSTRUCTIONS CAREFULLY.

Name: _____   Date: _____

1.	Ⓐ Ⓑ Ⓒ Ⓓ		24.	Ⓐ Ⓑ Ⓒ Ⓓ
2.	Ⓐ Ⓑ Ⓒ Ⓓ		25.	Ⓐ Ⓑ Ⓒ Ⓓ
3.	Ⓐ Ⓑ Ⓒ Ⓓ		26.	Ⓐ Ⓑ Ⓒ Ⓓ
4.	Ⓐ Ⓑ Ⓒ Ⓓ		27.	Ⓐ Ⓑ Ⓒ Ⓓ
5.	Ⓐ Ⓑ Ⓒ Ⓓ		28.	Ⓐ Ⓑ Ⓒ Ⓓ
6.	Ⓐ Ⓑ Ⓒ Ⓓ		29.	Ⓐ Ⓑ Ⓒ Ⓓ
7.	Ⓐ Ⓑ Ⓒ Ⓓ		30.	Ⓐ Ⓑ Ⓒ Ⓓ
8.	Ⓐ Ⓑ Ⓒ Ⓓ		31.	Ⓐ Ⓑ Ⓒ Ⓓ
9.	Ⓐ Ⓑ Ⓒ Ⓓ		32.	Ⓐ Ⓑ Ⓒ Ⓓ
10.	Ⓐ Ⓑ Ⓒ Ⓓ		33.	Ⓐ Ⓑ Ⓒ Ⓓ
11.	Ⓐ Ⓑ Ⓒ Ⓓ		34.	Ⓐ Ⓑ Ⓒ Ⓓ
12.	Ⓐ Ⓑ Ⓒ Ⓓ		35.	Ⓐ Ⓑ Ⓒ Ⓓ
13.	Ⓐ Ⓑ Ⓒ Ⓓ		36.	Ⓐ Ⓑ Ⓒ Ⓓ
14.	Ⓐ Ⓑ Ⓒ Ⓓ		37.	Ⓐ Ⓑ Ⓒ Ⓓ
15.	Ⓐ Ⓑ Ⓒ Ⓓ		38.	Ⓐ Ⓑ Ⓒ Ⓓ
16.	Ⓐ Ⓑ Ⓒ Ⓓ		39.	Ⓐ Ⓑ Ⓒ Ⓓ
17	Ⓐ Ⓑ Ⓒ Ⓓ		40.	Ⓐ Ⓑ Ⓒ Ⓓ
18.	Ⓐ Ⓑ Ⓒ Ⓓ		41.	Ⓐ Ⓑ Ⓒ Ⓓ
19.	Ⓐ Ⓑ Ⓒ Ⓓ		42.	Ⓐ Ⓑ Ⓒ Ⓓ
20.	Ⓐ Ⓑ Ⓒ Ⓓ		43.	Ⓐ Ⓑ Ⓒ Ⓓ
21.	Ⓐ Ⓑ Ⓒ Ⓓ		44.	Ⓐ Ⓑ Ⓒ Ⓓ
22.	Ⓐ Ⓑ Ⓒ Ⓓ		45.	Ⓐ Ⓑ Ⓒ Ⓓ
23.	Ⓐ Ⓑ Ⓒ Ⓓ		46.	Ⓐ Ⓑ Ⓒ Ⓓ

Practice Test

1. _____ is the type of license required to operate and tow most types of automobiles.

   A. Economy Class B
   B. Commercial Class B
   C. Commercial Class A
   D. Commercial Class C

2. There are __ categories of the motorbike Class M license.

   A. 2
   B. 3
   C. 8
   D. 10

3. If you intend to operate a motorcycle and are under the age of 21, state law requires that you _____.

   A. Are able to ride a bicycle
   B. Pass a motorcycle skills test
   C. Pass a car skills test
   D. Have a driver's license first

4. Any driver engaged in an accident must notify the DMV as soon as possible and within:

   A. 2 days
   B. 3 days
   C. 6 days
   D. 10 days

5. When using a phone while driving, the best safety measure is:

   A. Having one hand on the phone and one hand on the wheel
   B. Texting the other person
   C. Using hands–free devices so you can keep both hands on the steering wheel
   D. Video calling the other person

6. While driving on a windy day, a dust storm crosses the freeway, making it hard to see. You should slow down and activate your:

   A. Headlights
   B. Taillight
   C. Fog light
   D. Torch

7. When getting ready to turn at a traffic light, you should:

   A. Wait until the light is red before turning
   B. Slow down or stop, if necessary, and then make the turn
   C. Change the gear to neutral before turning
   D. First look at your rearview mirror

8. Which of these vehicles must always stop before crossing railroad tracks?

   A. Cars
   B. Bikes
   C. Tank trucks marked with hazardous materials placards
   D. RVs

9. The street you are on is one-way. A left turn into a different one-way street is only permitted if:

    A. Traffic on the street moves to the left
    B. Traffic on the street moves to the right
    C. Traffic on the street moves to the center
    D. Traffic stops

10. What should you do when other drivers pass you in a passing zone?

    A. Maintain your position
    B. Maintain your speed
    C. A & B
    D. None of the above

11. You can see a big truck turning right in front of you onto a roadway with two lanes going in either direction. The vehicle:

    A. May have to swing wide to complete the right turn
    B. May turn like a normal sized vehicle
    C. Is not legally allowed to turn right on a two lane road
    D. May drive slowly

12. When is it acceptable to drive through a bike lane?

    A. When you are planning to turn right within 200 feet
    B. When you want to block the bicycle behind you
    C. During rush hours
    D. Never

13. When changing lanes on a motorway, you should:

   A. Signal for at least five seconds prior to changing lanes
   B. Cross several lanes at a time to avoid slowdowns
   C. Avoid driving over broken white lines and lane markings
   D. Stop your car and look both sides

14. Which of the following is true about the use of turn signals?

   A. You should never use both electric and hand signals
   B. If you signal for a lane change, other drivers must let you in
   C. You must always signal for lane changes
   D. You should not signal when parallel parking because it is not a turn

15. If you want to pass another car, you should:

   A. Not assume they will make space for you to return to your lane
   B. Assume they will let you pass if you use your turn signal
   C. Assume they will maintain constant speed
   D. Stick your hand out and point your arm down

16 Which of these is the correct lane change procedure?

   A. Signal, check your mirrors, and then change lanes
   B. Signal, check your mirrors, and look over your shoulder
   C. Check your mirrors, look over your shoulder, then change lanes
   D. Change without looking anywhere

17. Which of these statements is true about changing lanes?

 A. You only need to turn and look over right shoulder for lane changes to the right or left
 B. Look over your right shoulder for a right lane change and your left shoulder for a left lane change
 C. Vehicles with two outside mirrors do not have blind spots
 D. You can change without looking anywhere

18. You can always cross a single broken white or yellow line except:

 A. When you are interfering with traffic by doing so
 B. When you have more than 1 passenger in your vehicle
 C. When you are driving slower than traffic
 D. When you are driving

19. Travelling at 55 mph on a two-lane highway you decide to pass the car in front of you. To pass successfully, you must:

 A. Wait until solid double, yellow lines separate the lanes
 B. Increase your speed to at least 60 mph
 C. Have a large enough gap in front of you
 D. Wait until the car in front of you comes to a complete stop

20. You may cross double yellow lines to pass another vehicle if the:

 A. Vehicle in front of you moves to the right and lets you pass
 B. Yellow line next to your side of the road is broken
 C. Yellow line next to the other side of the road is broken
 D. Vehicle is a large truck

21. You must look for bicycle riders in the same lanes used by motor vehicles because they:

   A. Must ride facing oncoming traffic
   B. Illegally share lanes with motor vehicles
   C. Are entitled to share the road with you
   D. Are illegal

22. A flashing red light at an intersection means:

   A. Slow down and proceed with caution
   B. U–turn and proceed in the opposite direction
   C. Stop fully, then proceed when it is safe to do so
   D. Drive faster

23. You should not pass another vehicle:

   A. When someone is likely to enter or cross the road
   B. On a multilane one–way street
   C. When a broken, yellow line is on the left side of your lane
   D. When you are driving fast

24. A flashing red traffic light at an intersection means:

   A. Slow down before entering
   B. Stop before entering
   C. Stop and wait for the green light
   D. Drive fast

Practice Test

25. A flashing yellow light means:

   A. Slow down and proceed with caution
   B. Stop
   C. Accelerate
   D. Go

26. Flashing amber lights near the top of a school bus mean:

   A. The bus is driving slowly
   B. The bus is driving slower than normal, be extra cautious
   C. The bus is going for an emergency stop, be cautious
   D. The bus is stopping to load or unload children. Slow down and be prepared to stop

27. A green arrow showing a red light means:

   A. Yield to vehicles and pedestrians, then proceed carefully
   B. Stop
   C. You have the right–of–way
   D. You can drive faster

28. How can you prevent being blinded at night by approaching cars?

   A. Look to the left side of the road
   B. Close your eyes
   C. Look to the right side of the road
   D. Look at the center

29. How do you make your vehicle more visible in bad weather?

   A. Honk
   B. Turn on your headlights on
   C. Turn your interior lights on
   D. Turn on your taillights

30. This sign means:

   A. Pedestrians walking along the road ahead
   B. Pedestrian crossing ahead
   C. Pedestrians must not cross here
   D. Stop

31. If you have trouble seeing other vehicles because of dust or smoke blowing across the roadway, you should drive slower and turn on your:

   A. Headlights
   B. Parking lights
   C. Emergency flashers
   D. Fog lamps

32. An intersection is blocked by cars as you approach a green signal. What action should you take?

   A. Partially enter the intersection to establish your right-of-way
   B. Don't enter the intersection until you can get completely across
   C. Continue into the intersection and wait for traffic to clear
   D. Drive around to try to cut one of the vehicles

33. When being passed by another vehicle, you should:

    A. Brake hard
    B. Maintain a constant speed
    C. Speed up
    D. Stop

34. This sign means:

    A. Yield the right-of-way
    B. No passing zone
    C. Reduction in lanes
    D. Stop

35. There are two lanes of traffic heading in the same direction as you. Many cars are passing on the right as you travel in the left lane. If the person driving in front of you wants to go quicker, you should:

    A. Stay in your lane so you don't impede the flow of traffic
    B. Drive onto the left shoulder to let the other vehicles pass
    C. Move into the right lane when it is safe
    D. Stay away

36. Yellow lines separate:

    A. Traffic lanes on one-way streets
    B. Traffic moving in opposite directions on two-way roads
    C. All carpool lanes from regular traffic lanes
    D. Left lanes

37. From top to bottom, the following is the proper order for traffic lights:

A. Red, yellow, green
B. Red, green, yellow
C. Green, red, yellow
D. Blue, orange, brown

38. When turning left from the center lane, you may only travel with that center lane for _____ before turning.

A. 200 feet
B. 100 feet
C. 800 feet
D. 700 feet

39. This sign means:

A. Side road
B. Merge
C. Yield the right-of-way
D. Center

40. If you cannot see at least _____ in both directions before turning, a U-turn is prohibited.

A. 100 feet
B. 800 feet
C. 900 feet
D. 200 feet

41. What should you do if every light at an intersection is out?

    A. Treat it as a two way stop
    B. Treat it as a four-way stop
    C. Make a U-turn and find another path
    D. Drive freely

42. You wish to park uphill on a two-way street but there is no curb. What direction do your front wheels turn?

    A. Right towards the side of the road
    B. Left
    C. Center
    D. Top

43. How long in advance should you look for potential hazards on the road?

    A. 12-13 seconds
    B. 15 seconds
    C. 40 seconds
    D. 10 to 15 seconds

44. When operating a vehicle on a two-way, multilane street, you should:

    A. Drive alongside other vehicles
    B. Drive ahead or behind the other vehicles
    C. Turn on your high beams
    D. Maintain a speed of 20 mph

45. You are involved in a minor crash. There are no injuries, and only minor car damage. You should:

    A.   Move your vehicle out of the traffic lane, if possible
    B.   Continue driving since no one is hurt
    C.   Drive slowly
    D.   Shift to left lane

46. When reversing a skid, use _____ steering.

    A.   Fast
    B.   Hand-over-hand
    C.   Slow
    D.   Leg-over-leg

Answer Key

1.   C. Commercial Class A

2.   A. 2

3.   B. Pass a motorcycle skills test

4.   D. 10 days

5.   C. Use hands–free devices so you can keep both hands on the steering wheel

6.   A. Headlights

7.   B. Slow down or stop, if necessary, and then make the turn

8.   C. Tank trucks marked with hazardous materials placards

9.   A. Traffic on the street moves to the left

10.   C. A & B

11.   A. May have to swing wide to complete the right turn

12.   A. When you are planning to turn right within 200 feet

13.   A. Signal for at least five seconds prior to changing lanes

14.   C. You must always signal for lane changes

15.   A. Not assume they will make space for you to return to your lane

16.   B. Signal, check your mirrors, and look over your shoulder

17.   B. Look over your right shoulder for a right lane change and your left shoulder for a left lane change

18.   A. When you are interfering with traffic by doing so

19.   C. Have a large enough gap in front of you

20.   B. Yellow line next to your side of the road is broken

21.   C. Are entitled to share the road with you

22.   C. Stop fully, then proceed when it is safe to do so

23.   A. When someone is likely to enter or cross the road

24.   B. Stop before entering

25.   A. Slow down and proceed with caution

26.   D. The bus is stopping to load or unload children. Slow down and be prepared to stop

27.   A. Yield to vehicles and pedestrians, then proceed carefully

28.   C. Look to the right side of the road

29.   B. Turn on your headlights on

30.   B. Pedestrian crossing ahead

31.   A. Headlights

32.   B. Don't enter the intersection until you can get completely across

33.   B. Maintain a constant speed

34.   A. Yield the right-of-way

35.   C. Move into the right lane when it is safe

36.   B. Traffic moving in opposite directions on two-way roads

37.   A. Red, yellow, green

38.   A. 200 feet

39.   A. Side road

40.   D. 200 feet

41.   B. Treat it as a four-way stop

42.   A. Right towards the side of the road

43.   D. 10 to 15 seconds

44.   B. Drive ahead or behind the other vehicles

 Practice Test

45.   A. Move your vehicle out of the traffic lane, if possible

46.   B. Hand-over-hand

Resources

Road Signs

Road signs should be memorized in addition to their purpose and the driver's expected reaction upon seeing one. These signs are made to **regulate** the road, **guide** the driver, and **warn** people.

Traffic signs provide information to drivers on what to expect and do. In addition to memorizing the text or image within the sign, pay close attention to the colors and shapes.

Red signs tell the driver to yield or stop. Yellow signs are general warnings or disclaimers of caution ahead. Black and white signs inform the driver of laws and regulations. Blue signs guide the driver to places like gas stations, hotels, and campgrounds. Orange signs indicate that construction is happening and to expect temporary disruptions in lane availability. Brown signs guide the driver to national parks and scenic areas.

Stop signs come in the shape of an octagon. A pentagon is used exclusively in school zones. Diamond signs are used by warnings. Vertical rectangles are used to show regulations and horizontal rectangles are used to show direction or information.

Take time to familiarize yourself with the following road signs.

Stop

A red-and-white regulatory traffic sign. This is the only octagonal (8-sided) traffic sign, you can easily recognize it by both shape and color.

At an intersection controlled by a "STOP" sign, you must come to a complete stop and check for pedestrians and cross traffic. Yield to other traffic going through the intersection and any pedestrians crossing the street.

Four Way Stop

This road sign is placed at four way stop intersections and informs drivers that all entrances to this intersection are controlled by stop signs. The basic rules that govern the right-of-way at four way stop intersections are as following: the first vehicle to arrive at the intersection should be the first to leave; when two vehicles reach the intersection at the same time, the driver of the vehicle on left must yield to the driver of the vehicle on the right; if two vehicles are facing each other and are traveling straight through the intersection, both vehicles can go at the same time.

Stop Except Right Turn

This placard is used in conjunction with the "STOP SIGN" and allows drivers to make a right turn without coming to a complete stop.

Stop Here on Red

This sign is used when it is not clear where vehicles must stop at an intersection with traffic signals. If there is a stop line, stop right before the stop line.

Wrong Way

You are going the wrong way on an expressway exit ramp or highway. Do not drive past this sign. Turn around immediately.

Speed Limit

Speed limit signs are rectangular black and white signs which are used to show the established maximum and minimum speed limits. These signs may indicate special speed limits which apply at certain times, or under certain conditions, or to certain kinds of vehicles. You must not drive faster than the posted maximum speed limit.

Yield

Triangle signs mean yield. You must slow down to a speed that is reasonable for existing conditions cand stop if necessary. If you must stop, do so at a marked stop line, if it exists. After slowing or stopping, you must yield the right-of-way to other vehicles in the intersection or approaching closely on another roadway or auxiliary road leading into a major highway.

Yield to Oncoming Traffic

An additional placard that may accompany a yield sign. If you see this placard, you are required to yield the right-of-way to traffic traveling in the opposite direction.

Divided Highway

The "Divided Highway" sign means that the road you are on intersects with a divided highway which has a median or a guide rail. If you need to merge onto the divided highway, keep in mind that you can only turn right at the first roadway and you can only turn left at the second roadway.

Do Not Enter

A "Do Not Enter" sign is usually installed at the beginning of one-way streets and ramps and it prohibits drivers from entering a one-way roadway where traffic is moving in the opposite direction. A DO NOT ENTER traffic sign is usually installed together with the "WRONG WAY" sign.

Do Not Pass

The DO NOT PASS traffic sign tells you where passing is not permitted. Passing areas are based on how far you can see ahead. They consider unseen hazards such as hills and curves, intersections, driveways, and other places where a vehicle may enter the roadway. These signs, along with pavement markings, indicate where you can pass another vehicle, the beginning and ending of a passing zone, or where you may not pass. Where it is permitted to pass, you may do so only if it is safe. Be aware of road conditions and other vehicles. Also look for double solid lines on the highway.

Pass With Care

Pass with care signs are rectangular, black and white signs indicating the end of a no-passing zone. This road sign serves as a reminder that passing is allowed, provided you can do so safely.

Keep Right

While the look of the "KEEP RIGHT" sign may change from state to state, its meaning is always the same. The sign marks a traffic island or a highway divider and it warns you to stay to the right of the obstacle. When this sign is installed at a highway, it may also be accompanied by the "DIVIDED HIGHWAY BEGINS" yellow warning sign.

Left Turn Yield on Green

This road sign is installed at busy intersections to remind drivers that they can make a left turn on green signal, provided they yield to oncoming traffic. Some drivers make the mistake of waiting for a green arrow signal to appear to be able to make a turn. While turning on a green arrow signal does give you the right-of-way over oncoming traffic, since you are making a protected turn, you can still make a left turn on the regular green signal.

Resourc

No Bicycles

The "NO BICYCLES" sign forbids cyclists from entering a roadway where the sign is installed. In most cases, the sign is installed on high-speed roadways.

No Left Turn

This traffic sign indicates that left turns are prohibited. When you see the "NO LEFT TURN" sign at an intersection, you can either travel straight through or turn right.

No Left Turn on Red

This traffic sign prohibits left turns during the red-light cycle at an intersection. You must wait for the green signal before making the turn.

No Parking

You may not park at locations where this sign is installed. Some states use additional pavement markings to inform drivers of parking restrictions in the area.

No Pedestrian Crossing

The "NO PEDESTRIAN CROSSING" sign forbids pedestrians to cross the street in this place.

No Right Turn

Do not make a right turn at an intersection marked by the "NO RIGHT TURN" sign. You can either travel straight or turn left.

No Trucks

The "NO TRUCKS" sign forbids large trucks from entering a roadway where the sign is installed.

No Turn on Red

This road sign prohibits drivers from making turns during the red-light cycle. Keep in mind that this sign prohibits both left and right turns. You need to wait until the traffic signal changes to green before making a turn.

No Right Turn on Red

This traffic sign prohibits right turns during the red-light cycle at an intersection. You must wait for the green signal before making the turn.

No U-turn

This road sign prohibits U-turns. You can make a left turn at this intersection, but making a complete turn to go in the opposite direction is not allowed.

One Way

This sign warns you that you are crossing a one-way street and that you can only make a turn in the direction the arrow is pointing.

Opposing Traffic Extended Green

This road sign is placed where opposing traffic may continue to move through the intersection after your signal has turned red.

Resource

Railroad Crossbuck

The railroad crossbuck sign is placed at railroad crossings where the tracks cross the roadway. The crossbuck sign can be treated in the same manner as a YIELD sign: slow down, listen for trains and be prepared to stop if you see or hear a train approaching.

Railroad Crossing Gate

Gates are used with flashing light signals at some crossings. Stop when the lights begin to flash and before the gate lowers. Remain stopped until the gates are raised and the lights stop flashing. Do not attempt to drive around the lowered gate. Also, pedestrians may not cross railroad tracks when warned of a train by an automatic signal, crossing gates, flagman or law enforcement officer.

Reserved Parking

This sign marks areas where parking is reserved for disabled drivers. When parking in the space marked by the "RESERVERD PARKING" sign, a special parking placard or authorized registration plates must be displayed on the vehicle.

Right Turn Signal

This sign is posted close to a traffic signal to indicate the the signal controls right turn movements.

Center Turn Lane

The center lane is shared for left turns in both directions of travel. Traveling or passing in the center turn lane is forbidden.

Lane Use Control Sign

Lane use control signs are rectangular, black and white signs indicating that turning movements are required or the unusual turning movements are permitted from specific lanes at an intersection. You must move your vehicle only in the direction indicated for your traffic lane.

Straight or Turn Right

This sign lets you know that your lane is splitting off into two separate directions. From this lane, you can travel straight through the intersection or turn right.

Turn Left Only

When you are traveling in the lane marked with this road sign, you know that you are in a dedicated turn lane and you are only allowed to travel in the direction the arrow is pointing in. The road sign is usually accompanied by similar pavement markings, a white arrow on the pavement pointing in the direction of the turn. Left turns only are allowed from the lane displaying this sign.

Turn Left or Right

Left and right turns are allowed from this lane. Traveling straight is forbidden.

Turn Right Only

One of the regulatory lane use control signs. The "Turn right only" road sign marks dedicated turn lanes. Right turns only are allowed from the lane displaying this sign.

Restricted Lane Ahead

A diamond-shaped marking shows that a lane is reserved for certain purposes or certain vehicles. The lanes are usually reserved for buses or car-pool vehicles during rush hour traffic.

Emergency Stopping Only

Stopping in the area marked by the "EMERGENCY STOPPING ONLY" traffic sign is permitted only for real emergencies, i.e., when you have technical troubles with the vehicle that may impact your safety or when you have a medical emergency.

No Turns

You may not turn neither right nor left at an intersection marked by the "NO TURNS" sign. Traveling straight through the intersection is your only option.

Minimum Speed Limit

The "MINIMUM SPEED LIMIT" traffic sign displays minimum speed you are allowed to travel on the road. In some cases, the maximum and minimum speed limits are displayed on a single sign.

Speed Limit - Maximum & Minimum

This traffic sign shows the "maximum" and "minimum" speeds permitted on this section of the highway. Road signs with minimum and maximum speed limits are usually posted on freeways and other controlled access highways.

Speed Limit - Children

School zone speed limit, active only when children are present. Slow down to posted speed limit if you see children near the roadway. In some states, the posted speed limit applies only on school days when children are present (usual school hours are 7 a.m. to 4 p.m., but hours may vary).

Speed Limit Lights Flashing

Speed limit in the school zone. Do not exceed the posted speed limit when lights are flashing and be on the lookout for children near the road.

Road Closed

Road closed to all traffic. Detour.

Slower Traffic Keep Right

This sign is posted for those driving slower than the normal speed of traffic on a multilane highways. It reminds slow drivers to drive in the right lane.

Bump

The traffic sign warns you that there is a bump up ahead on the road. Reduce speed and make sure to have both hands on the steering wheel as you approach the bump to avoid losing control of the vehicle.

No Passing Zone

This pennant-shaped yellow and black traffic sign marks the beginning of a no passing zone. The sign is placed on the left side of the road, facing the driver. You may not pass cars ahead of you in your lane. If you started passing another vehicle and you see the sign up ahead on the road, you must complete passing before you enter the no passing zone.

Resource

Chevron Signs

This sign warns you of a change in direction or narrowing of the road. You may find several of these signs on the outside of a sharp curve or on approaches to a narrow bridge.

Advisory Speed

These cautionary signs show the safe speed around curves, corners, and off-ramps. It is often posted under other warning signs that warn you of the nature of the danger ahead. Keep in mind that advisory speed signs display recommended speed under ideal conditions. If the road is slippery and is covered in ice, snow or water, you should reduce your speed even further to negotiate the turn or the curve safely.

Merging Traffic

Traffic may be merging into your lane from another roadway. Be ready to either changes lanes or allow other traffic to merge into your lane. Merge signs appear on expressways just before expressway ramps. Drivers entering from the right must yield to traffic on the main route, and must make use of speed-change lanes to merge smoothly and safely with the main traffic flow.

Added Lane

Added lane, merging not required, watch for other vehicles changing lanes.

Weave Area

This sign is used to warn that you will be merging with another roadway as some traffic is exiting and crossing your path. In most cases, it is installed at highway interchanges that don't have dedicated merge and exit lanes.

Divided Highway Begins

The highway ahead is split into two separate roadways by a median or divider and each roadway is one-way. Keep to the right.

Divided Highway Ends

The divided highway on which you are traveling ends 350 to 500 feet ahead. You will then be on a roadway with two-way traffic. Keep to the right of approaching traffic.

Two Way Traffic Ahead

You are leaving a separated one-way roadway and entering a two-way roadway. Also used to remind drivers they are on a two-way road.

Lane Ends Ahead

This sign is used on multi-lane highways to warn you of a reduction in the number of traffic lanes in the direction you are traveling. Be prepared to change lanes or to allow other vehicles to merge into your lane.

Slippery When Wet

When pavement is wet, reduce your speed. Do not brake hard or change direction suddenly, if you need to negotiate a sharp turn, do so slowly. Increase the distance between your car and the one ahead. These actions are needed on all wet roads and especially on roads where this sign is posted.

Resourc

Railroad Crossing Ahead

A round yellow warning sign with an "X" symbol and black "RR" letters. This sign is posted a few hundred feet in front of the tracks and alerts you to slow down, look, listen and prepare to stop. If necessary, roll down a window and listen carefully for an approaching train. If a train is approaching, stop! Do not try to calculate whether you can "make it" across the track. Never try to beat a train through the intersection. Passing is prohibited at all railroad crossings.

School Zone

Five-sided sign back on yellow is used only to warn of schools and school crossings. Slow down – school zones have a speed limit you must observe. Watch out for children crossing the street or playing. Be ready to stop. Obey signals from any crossing guards. New fluorescent yellow-green signs may also be used.

School Crossing Ahead

Signs may display horizontal lines indicating the point where a crosswalk exists. School zone crosswalk traffic signs may have a separate downward-pointing arrow plaque, which indicates the actual location of the crosswalk.

Traffic Signal Ahead

Slow down and be prepared to come to a complete stop on red signal.

Left Curve

The roadway ahead curves to the left. Slow your speed and keep well to the right.
The sign may be accompanied by an advisory speed placard, helping you navigate the curve safely.

Right Curve

The roadway ahead curves to the right. Slow your speed and keep well to the left.

Sharp Left Turn

The road will make a sharp turn to the left. Slow your speed, keep to the left and do not pass other vehicles.

Sharp Right Turn

The road will make a sharp turn to the right. Slow your speed, keep to the right, and do not pass other vehicles.

Set of Curves (Left-Right)

There is a series of curves up ahead on the road. The road will first curve to the left and then to the right. The sign is frequently accompanied by a placard that indicates recommended speed for the curve. Slow down to negotiate these curves safely.

Set of Curves (Right-Left)

There is a series of curves up ahead on the road. The road will first curve to the right and then to the left. The sign is frequently accompanied by a placard that indicates recommended speed for the curve. Slow down to negotiate these curves safely.

Sharp Turns (Left-Right)

There is a series of sharp turns up ahead on the road. The road will first turn to the left and then to the right. The sign is frequently accompanied by a placard that indicates recommended speed for these turns. Slow down to negotiate sharp turns safely.

Sharp Turns (Right-Left)

There is a series of sharp turns up ahead on the road. The road will first turn to the right and then to the left. The sign is frequently accompanied by a placard that indicates recommended speed for these turns. Slow down to negotiate sharp turns safely.

Winding Road

WINDING ROAD (SET OF CURVES). This sign indicates there are three (3) or more curves in a row on the road ahead. The sign is frequently accompanied by an advisory speed sign. Slow down to recommended speed before you enter the curves.

One Direction Arrow

The road ahead changes direction at an extreme angle. Before you reach such an extreme curve, slow down as much as you would to make a turn at an intersection.

Road Entering Curve

The main road curves to the left with a side road entering from the right. Approach the intersection with extra caution. A driver preparing to enter the main road may not be able to see you approaching from around the curve and may pull out in front of you, leaving you little room to avoid a crash, if you are traveling too fast.

Truck Rollover

This sign identifies curves where trucks traveling at excessive speeds have a potential to rollover.

Road Narrows

This traffic sign warns you that the road ahead is not as wide as the road you are currently traveling on. The "ROAD NARROWS" sign is frequently used along with other warning signs that provide additional information regarding the danger, such as "LANE ENDS AHEAD" or "LANE ENDS MERGE".

Pavement Ends

The road surface ahead changes from a hard-surfaced pavement to a low-type surface or earth road. Slow down and check vehicle control on changed surface.

Lane Ends Merge Left

The "Lane Ends Merge" tells you that one of the lanes on a multi-lane roadway will end ahead. In this example, the traffic in the right lane must merge left.

Left Lane Ends

The "Left Lane Ends" traffic sign tells you that left lane on roadway will end ahead. You are required to merge right. This road sign is frequently installed in advance of the upcoming road work zone.

Cross Road

One of the intersection traffic signs. Another road crosses the highway ahead. Look left and right for other traffic. Be alert for cross traffic and regulatory signals.

Resourc

Side Road

Side road enters highway from right. One of the warning intersection traffic signs that can help you navigate an approaching intersection.

T Intersection

One of the intersection traffic signs. The road you are traveling on ends straight ahead. Slow down and prepare to stop before turning. Most T-intersections will feature a YIELD sign or a STOP sign to remind you to give the right-of-way to cross traffic.

Y Intersection

One of the intersection traffic signs. There is a three-way intersection up ahead on the road, with all roads being of equal size and importance.

Roundabout

A roundabout is a circular intersection that usually does not include a traffic signal and flows in a counter-clockwise direction around a central island. Motorists must enter from the right - yielding to traffic already in the roundabout - and follow the circle to the right.

Two Direction Arrow

This sign is placed at the intersection. Yield the right-of-way or stop before turning right or left. You cannot travel straight through the intersection and must turn either right or left.

Narrow Bridge Ahead

Narrow bridge or overpass ahead. Room for two lanes of traffic but potentially dangerous. Slow down and watch out for oncoming vehicles.

Watch for Ice on Bridges

This traffic sign is usually installed if there is a bridge ahead and serves as a reminder to drivers that ice may form on the bridge even if the rest of the road is not covered in ice or snow. Slow down whenever the weather requires it.

Deer Crossing

Watch for deer crossing the road.

Low Clearance

When a bridge has an overhead clearance less than 14 feet, this sign is posted indicating the actual legal overhead clearance of a bridge or elevated structure. Do not enter if your vehicle is taller than the height listed.

Bicycle Crossing

The bicycle crossing sign provides you with an early warning that the road you are traveling on will have cyclists crossing up ahead. Slow down and be on the look-out for cyclists entering and exiting the road.

Pedestrian Crossing

Watch for people crossing the street. Slow down or stop if necessary. Remember that people crossing the street on the pedestrian crossing have the right-of-way. Slowing down is important since pedestrians may be obscured by parked vehicles and you may not see them the moment, they enter the roadway.

Resource

Dip

There is a low place up ahead in on the road. In most situations, a dip in the road is harmless. However, you have to watch out for low areas of the road when it is raining or just after the rain. Water may accumulate in the dip and driving through the water at high speeds may cause hydroplaning, a condition when water accumulates under the tire and you lose control of the vehicle.

Hill / Downgrade

This traffic sign warns you about a hill or a downgrade up ahead on the road. Slow down and be ready to shift to lower gear to control speed and save brakes. Remember that making U-turns and passing other vehicles on hills is forbidden, these maneuvers become dangerous due to low visibility.

Shoulder Drop Off

This sign is used where the shoulder is more than three inches below the level of the road. If you stray off the roadway and one wheel drops off onto a low shoulder or a soft shoulder, do not slam on the brakes of steer sharply to try to get back onto the roadway – you can easily lose control of your vehicle!

Island Ahead

Indicates traffic is permitted to pass on either side of a traffic island or an obstruction.

Cross Traffic

Slow down and watch for cross traffic. Look carefully in all directions for traffic.

Highway Intersection Ahead

The road you are traveling on intersects a highway ahead. Slow down, look to the right and to the left for other traffic, be prepared to stop and yield to crossing traffic.

Loose Gravel

The surface of the road is covered with loose gravel. Go slow enough to keep complete control of your vehicle. Do not apply brakes suddenly or make sharp turns as this may cause a skid.

Highway Guide Sign

Highway guide signs are green with white letters. Most highway and expressway signs are posted the same way. For example, there is usually one advance sign which is followed by another advance sign. The third sign then is posted at the exit. Several signs are necessary because the high speed and heavy traffic on highways can cause drivers to miss seeing a single sign.

Diesel

One of the service traffic signs, the diesel traffic sign informs drivers that there is a gas station nearby that has diesel fuel available.

Mile Markers

Milepost markers are placed each mile along the edge of the roadway from one end of the state to the other. Zero always starts at south or west border where a route begins.

Resourc

Exit Only Highway Sign

If a yellow panel with the message EXIT ONLY is on a highway sign, the lane below the sign will not continue through the interchange; instead, the lane will go off of the road to form a ramp. If you are in a lane posted with an EXIT ONLY, you may change lanes, or you must exit the highway if you stay in this lane.

Hospital

Hospital signs let you know that there is a medical establishment nearby. These service signs are frequently accompanied by a placard that points in the direction you need to take to reach the hospital.

Active Work Zone

This sign is placed at the beginning of an active work zone. An active work zone is the portion of a work zone where construction, maintenance or utility workers are on the roadway, or on the shoulder of the highway next to an open travel lane.

End of Active Work Zone

This sign is placed at the end of an active work zone. An active work zone is the portion of a work zone where construction, maintenance or utility workers are on the roadway, or on the shoulder of the highway next to an open travel lane.

Road Work Ahead

This sign informs you there is road work ahead and also cautions you to slow down.

Workers Ahead

One of the work zone road signs. Workers may on or are very close to the roadway, so take special care when traveling through the area. Be prepared to reduce your speed and use caution when directed to do so by a sign, flagger and/or police officer.

Flagger Ahead

The sign is also known as ROAD CONSTRUCTION AHEAD. This traffic signs warns you that a flagger is controlling traffic ahead. Flaggers use STOP and SLOW paddles or a red flag to signal traffic to stop or slow down. Pay special attentions to flaggers when approaching and traveling through a work zone.

Work Zone Headlights

Work Zone Signs are normally diamond shaped, like warning signs, but they are orange with black lettering instead of yellow with black lettering. These signs identify maintenance, construction or utility areas where workers or equipment may be on or near the roadway. Stay alert and slow down when you see these signs.

Single Broken Yellow Line

A single, broken yellow centerline shows the center of a two-way, two-lane road. Passing is permitted on either side, if safe conditions exist. When passing, you must use the lane belonging to oncoming traffic.

Double Solid Yellow Line

A double, solid yellow centerline shows the center of a two-way road. Even if it is not marked with a NO PASSING sign, passing by traffic traveling in either direction is not allowed on roads marked in this manner.

Resource

Center Turning Lane

Marking patterns like the ones shown in the picture may be found on many three-lane highways. The solid yellow centerline means you cannot use the center lane for passing. The broken yellow centerlines show that vehicles traveling in either direction may use the center lane only to make left turns. A two-way left turning lane is a dedicated turn lane, make sure to use it as such.

Solid Yellow and Broken Yellow Centerline

The combination of a solid yellow and a broken yellow centerline also shows the center of a two-way roadway. You may pass if the broken line is on your side of the road and safe conditions exist, but you may not pass when a solid yellow line is on your side of the road.

Made in the USA
Las Vegas, NV
07 January 2024

84060431R00059